Book 1
C Programming Professional
Made Easy

BY SAM KEY

&

Book 2
C++ Programming Professional
Made Easy

BY SAM KEY

Book 1
C Programming Professional Made Easy

BY SAM KEY

Expert C Programming Language Success In A Day For Any Computer User!

**Programming Box Set #18: C Programming Professional Made Easy & C++
Programming Professional Made Ease**

Table Of Contents

Introduction

I want to thank you and congratulate you for purchasing the book, "Professional C Programming Made Easy: Expert C Programming Language Success In A Day For Any Computer User!".

This book contains proven steps and strategies on how to understand and perform C programming. C is one of the most basic programming tools used for a wide array of applications. Most people stay away from it because the language seem complicated, with all those characters, letters, sequences and special symbols.

This book will break down every element and explain in detail each language used in the C program. By the time you are done with this book, C programming language will be easy to understand and easy to execute.

Read on and learn.

Thanks again for purchasing this book. I hope you enjoy it!

Chapter 1 The Basic Elements Of C

The seemingly complicated C program is composed of the following basic elements:

Character Set

The alphabet in both upper and lower cases is used in C. The 0-9 digits are also used, including white spaces and some special characters. These are used in different combinations to form elements of a basic C program such as expressions, constants, variables, etc.

Special characters include the following:

> + ,. *– / % = & ! #?"^ '| / ()< > { } [ ];: @ ~!

White spaces include:

- Blank space

- Carriage return

- Horizontal tab

- Form feed

- New line

Identifiers

An identifier is a name given to the various elements of the C program, such as arrays, variables and functions. These contain digits and letters in various arrangements. However, identifiers should always start with a letter. The letters may be in upper case, lower case or both. However, these are not interchangeable. C programming is case sensitive, as each letter in different cases is regarded as separate from each other. Underscores are also permitted because it is considered by the program as a kind of letter.

Examples of valid identifiers include the following:

ab123

A

stud_name

average

velocity

TOTAL

Identifiers need to start with a letter and should not contain illegal characters. Examples of invalid identifiers include the following:

2nd — should always start with a letter

"Jamshedpur" — contains the illegal character (")

stud name — contains a blank space, which is an illegal character

stud-name — contains an illegal character (-)

In C, a single identifier may be used to refer to a number of different entities within the same C program. For instance, an array and a variable can share one identifier. For example:

The variable is int difference, average, A[5]; // sum, average

The identifier is A[5].

In the same program, an array can be named A, too.

__func__

The __func__ is a predefined identifier that provides functions names and makes these accessible and ready for use anytime in the function. The complier would automatically declare the __func__ immediately after placing the opening brace when declaring the function definitions. The compiler declares the predefined identifier this way:

static const char _ _func_ _[] = "Alex";

"Alex" refers to a specific name of this particular function.

Take a look at this example:

```c
#include <stdio.h>


void anna1(void)   {

    printf("%sn",__func__);

    return;

}


int main() {

    myfunc();

}
```

What will appear as an output will be anna1

Keywords

Reserved words in C that come with standard and predefined meanings are called keywords. The uses for these words are restricted to their predefined intended purpose. Keywords cannot be utilized as programmer-defined identifiers. In C, there are 32 keywords being used, which include the following:

auto	default
break	double
char	float
case	else
continue	extern
const	enum
do	goto

for	switch
if	typedef
long	struct
int	union
register	switch
short	void
return	unsigned
sizeof	while
signed	volatile

Data Types

There are different types of data values that are passed in C. Each of the types of data has different representations within the memory bank of the computer. These also have varying memory requirements. Data type modifiers/qualifiers are often used to augment the different types of data.

Supported data types in C include int, char, float, double, void, _Bool, _Complex, arrays, and constants.

int

Integer quantities are stored in this type of data. The data type *int* can store a collection of different values, starting from INT_MAX to INT_MIN. An in-header file, <limits h>, defines the range.

These int data types use type modifiers such as unsigned, signed, long, long long and short.

Short int means that they occupy memory space of only 2 bytes.

A long int uses 4 bytes of memory space.

Short unsigned int is a data type that uses 2 bytes of memory space and store positive values only, ranging from 0 to 65535.

Unsigned int requires memory space similar to that of short unsigned int. For regular and ordinary int, the bit at the leftmost portion is used for the integer's sign.

Long unsigned int uses 4 bytes of space. It stores all positive integers ranging from 0 to 4294967295.

An int data is automatically considered as signed.

Long long int data type uses 64 bits memory. This type may either be unsigned or signed. Signed long long data type can store values ranging from −9,223,372,036,854,775,808 to 9,223,372,036,854,775,807. Unsigned long long data type stores value range of 0 to 18,446,744,073,709,551,615.

char

Single characters such as those found in C program's character set are stored by this type of data. The char data type uses 1 byte in the computer's memory. Any value from C program's character set can be stored as char. Modifiers that can be used are either unsigned or signed.

A char would always use 1 byte in the computer's memory space, whether it is signed or unsigned. The difference is on the value range. Values that can be stored as unsigned char range from 0 to 255. Signed char stores values ranging from −128 to +127. By default, a char data type is considered unsigned.

For each of the char types, there is a corresponding integer interpretation. This makes each char a special short integer.

float

A float is a data type used in storing real numbers that have single precision. That is, precision denoted as having 6 more digits after a decimal point. Float data type uses 4 bytes memory space.

The modifier for this data type is long, which uses the same memory space as that of double data type.

double

The double data type is used for storing real numbers that have double precision. Memory space used is 8 bytes. Double data type uses long as a type modifier. This uses up memory storage space of 10 bytes.

void

Void data type is used for specifying empty sets, which do not contain any value. Hence, void data type also occupies no space (0 bytes) in the memory storage.

_Bool

This is a Boolean type of data. It is an unsigned type of integer. It stores only 2 values, which is 0 and 1. When using _Bool, include **<stdboolh>**.

_Complex

This is used for storing complex numbers. In C, three types of _Complex are used. There is the float _Complex, double _Complex, and long double _Complex. These are found in <complex h> file.

Arrays

This identifier is used in referring to the collection of data that share the same name and of the same type of data. For example, all integers or all characters that have the same name. Each of the data is represented by its own array element. The subscripts differentiate the arrays from each other.

Constants

Constants are identifiers used in C. The values of identifiers do not change anywhere within the program. Constants are declared this way:

const datatype varname = value

const is the keyword that denotes or declares the variable as the fixed value entity, i.e., the constant.

In C, there are 4 basic constants used. These include the integer constant, floating-point, character and string constants. Floating-point and integer types of constant do not contain any blank spaces or commas. Minus signs can be used, which denotes negative quantities.

Integer Constants

Integer constants are integer valued numbers consisting of sequence of digits. These can be written using 3 different number systems, namely, decimal, octal and hexadecimal.

Decimal system (base 10)

An integer constant written in the decimal system contains combinations of numbers ranging from 0 to 9. Decimal constants should start with any number other except 0. For example, a decimal constant is written in C as:

const int size =76

Octal (base 8)

Octal constants are any number combinations from 0 to 7. To identify octal constants, the first number should be 0. For example:

const int a= 043; const int b=0;

An octal constant is denoted in the binary form. Take the octal 0347. Each digit is represented as:

$0347 = 011\ 100\ 111 = 3 * 8^2 + 4 * 8^1 + 7 * 8^0 = 231$
--- --- ---
3 4 7

Hexadecimal constant (base 16)

This type consists of any of the possible combinations of digits ranging from 0 to 9. This type also includes letters a to f, written in either lowercase or uppercase. To identify hexadecimal constants, these should start with 0X or 0X. For example:

const int c= 0x7FF;

For example, the hexadecimal number 0x2A5 is internally represented in bit patterns within C as:

$0x2A5 = 0010\ 1010\ 0101 = 2 * 16^2 + 10 * 16^1 + 5 * 16^0 = 677$
---- ---- ----
2   A 5

Wherein, 677 is the decimal equivalent of the hexadecimal number 0x2.

Prefixes for integer constants can either be long or unsigned. A long integer constant (long int) ends with a l of L, such as 67354L or 67354l. The last portion of an unsigned long integer constant should either be ul or UL, such as 672893UL or 672893ul. For an unsigned long long integer constant, UL or ul should be at the last portion. An unsigned constant should end with U or u, such as 673400095u or 673400095U. Normal integer constants are written without any suffix, such as a simple 67458.

Floating Point Constant

This type of constant has a base 10 or base 16 and contains an exponent, a decimal point or both. For a floating point constant with a base 10 and a decimal point, the base is replaced by an E or e. For example, the constant $1.8 *10^-3$ is written as 1.8e-3 or 1.8E-3.

For hexadecimal character constants and the exponent is in the binary form, the exponent is replaced by P or p. Take a look at this example:

This type of constant is often precision quantities. These occupy around 8 bytes of memory. Different add-ons are allowed in some C program versions, such as F for a single precision floating constant or L for a long floating point type of constant.

Character Constant

A sequence of characters, whether single or multiple ones, enclosed by apostrophes or single quotation marks is called a character constant. The character set in the computer determines the integer value equivalent to each character constant. Escape sequences may also be found within the sequence of a character constant.

Single character constants enclosed by apostrophes is internally considered as integers. For example, 'A' is a single character constant that has an integer value of 65. The corresponding integer value is also called the ASCII value. Because of the corresponding numerical value, single character constants can be used in calculations just like how integers are used. Also, these constants can also be used when comparing other types of character constants.

Prefixes used in character constants such as L, U or u are used for character literals. These are considered as wide types of character constants. Character literals with the prefix L are considered under the type wchar_t, which are defined as <stddef.h> under the header file. Character constants that use the prefix U or u are considered as type char16_t or char32_t. These are considered as unsigned types of characters and are defined under the header file as <uchar.h>.

Those that do not have the prefix L are considered a narrow or ordinary character constant. Those that have escape sequences or are composed of at least 2 characters are considered as multicharacter constants.

Escape sequences are a type of character constant used in expressing non-printing characters like carriage return or tab. This sequence always begins with a backward slash, followed by special characters. These sequences represent a single character in the C language even if they are composed of more than 1 character. Examples of some of the most common escape sequences, and their integer (ASCII) value, used in C include the following:

Character	Escape Sequence	ASCII Value
Backspace	\b	008
Bell	\a	007
Newline	\n	010
Null	\o	000
Carriage	\r	013
Horizontal tab	\t	009
Vertical tab	\v	011
Form feed	\f	012

String Literals

Multibyte characters that form a sequence are called string literals. Multibyte characters have bit representations that fit into 1 or more bytes. String literals are enclosed within double quotation marks, for example, "A" and "Anna". There are 2 types of string literals, namely, UTF-8 string literals and wide string literals. Prefixes used for wide string literals include u, U or L. Prefix for UTF-8 string literals is u8.

Additional characters or extended character sets included in string literals are recognized and supported by the compiler. These additional characters can be used meaningfully to further enhance character constants and string literals.

14

Symbolic constants

Symbolic constants are substitute names for numeric, string or character constants within a program. The compiler would replace the symbolic constants with its actual value once the program is run.

At the beginning of the program, the symbolic constant is defined with a **#define** feature. This feature is called the preprocessor directive.

The definition of a symbolic constant does not end with a semi colon, like other C statements. Take a look at this example:

> #define PI 3.1415

> (//PI is the constant that will represent value 3.1415)

> #define True 1

> #define name "Alice"

For all numeric constants such as floating point and integer, non-numeric characters and blank spaces are not included. These constants are also limited by minimum and maximum bounds, which are usually dependent on the computer.

Variables

Memory locations where data is stored are called variables. These are indicated by a unique identifier. Names for variables are symbolic representations that refer to a particular memory location. Examples are *count, car_no* and *sum.*

Rules when writing the variable names

Writing variable names follow certain rules in order to make sure that data is stored properly and retrieved efficiently.

- Letters (in both lowercase and uppercase), underscore ('_') and digits are the only characters that can be used for variable names.

- Variables should begin either with an underscore or a letter. Starting with an underscore is acceptable, but is not highly recommended. Underscores at the beginning of variables can come in conflict with system names and the compiler may protest.

- There is no limit on the length of variables. The compiler can distinguish the first 31 characters of a variable. This means that individual variables should have different sequences for the 1st 31 characters.

Variables should also be declared at the beginning of a program before it can be used.

Chapter 2 What is C Programming Language?

In C, the programming language is a language that focuses on the structure. It was developed in 1972, at Bell Laboratories, by Dennis Ritchie. The features of the language were derived from "B", which is an earlier programming language and formally known as BCPL or Basic Combined Programming Language. The C programming language was originally developed to implement the UNIX operating system.

Standards of C Programming Language

In 1989, the American National Standards Institute developed the 1st standard specifications. This pioneering standard specification was referred to as C89 and C90, both referring to the same programming language.

In 1999, a revision was made in the programming language. The revised standard was called C99. It had new features such as advanced data types. It also had a few changes, which gave rise to more applications.

The C11 standard was developed, which added new features to the programming language for C. This had a library-like generic macro type, enhanced Unicode support, anonymous structures, multi-threading, bounds-checked functions and atomic structures. It had improved compatibility with C++. Some parts of the C99 library in C11 were made optional.

The Embedded C programming language included a few features that were not part of C. These included the named address spaces, basic I/O hardware addressing and fixed point arithmetic.

C Programming Language Features

There are a lot of features of the programming language, which include the following:

- Modularity

- Interactivity

- Portability

- Reliability

- Effectiveness

- Efficiency

- Flexibility

Uses of the C Programming Language

This language has found several applications. It is now used for the development of system applications, which form a huge portion of operating systems such as Linux, Windows and UNIX.

Some of the applications of C language include the following:

- Spreadsheets

- Database systems

- Word processors

- Graphics packages

- Network drivers

- Compilers and Assemblers

- Operating system development

- Interpreters

Chapter 3 Understanding C Program

The C program has several features and steps in order for an output or function is carried out.

Basic Commands (for writing basic C Program)

The basic syntax and commands used in writing a simple C program include the following:

#include <stdio.h>

This command is a preprocessor. <stdio.h> stands for standard input output header file. This is a file from the C library, which is included before the C program is compiled.

int main()

Execution of all C program begins with this main function.

{

This symbol is used to indicate the start of the main function.

}

This indicates the conclusion of the main function.

/* */

Anything written in between this command will not be considered for execution and compilation.

printf (output);

The printf command prints the output on the screen.

getch();

Writing this command would allow the system to wait for any keyboard character input.

return 0

Writing this command will terminate the C program or main function and return to 0.

A basic C Program would look like this:

```
#include <stdio.h>
int main()
{
/* Our first simple C basic program */
printf("Hello People! ");
getch();
return 0;
}
```

The output of this simple program would look like this:

Hello People!

Chapter 4 Learn C Programming

After learning the basic elements and what the language is all about, time to start programming in C. Here are the most important steps:

Download a compiler

A compiler is a program needed to compile the C code. It interprets the written codes and translates it into specific signals, which can be understood by the computer. Usually, compiler programs are free. There are different compilers available for several operating systems. Microsoft Visual Studio and MinGW are compilers available for Windows operating systems. XCode is among the best compilers for Mac. Among the most widely used C compiler options for Linux is gcc.

Basic Codes

Consider the following example of a simple C program in the previous chapter:

```
#include <stdio.h>

int main()

{

    printf("Hello People!\n");

    getchar();

    return 0;

}
```

At the start of the program, #include command is placed. This is important in order to load the libraries where the needed functions are located.

The <stdio.h> refers to the file library and allows for the use of the succeeding functions getchar() and printf().

The command int main () sends a message to the compiler to run the function with the name "main" and return a certain integer once it is done running. Every C program executes a main function.

The symbol { } is used to specify that everything within it is a component of the "main" function that the compiler should run.

The function printf() tells the system to display the words or characters within the parenthesis onto the computer screen. The quotation marks make certain that the C compiler would print the words or characters as it is. The sequence \n informs the C compiler to place its cursor to the succeeding line. At the conclusion of the line, a ; (semicolon) is placed to denote that the sequence is done. Most codes in C program needs a semicolon to denote where the line ends.

The command getchar() informs the compiler to stop once it reaches the end of the function and standby for an input from the keyboard before continuing. This command is very useful because most compilers would run the C program and then immediately exits the window. The getchar() command would prevent the compiler to close the window until after a keystroke .is made.

The command return o denotes that the function has ended. For this particular C program, it started as an int, which indicates that the program has to return an integer once it is done running. The "o" is an indication that the compiler ran the program correctly. If another number is returned at the end of the program, it means that there was an error somewhere in the program.

Compiling the program

To compile the program, type the code into the program's code editor. Save this as a type of *.c file, then click the Run or Build button.

Commenting on the code

Any comments placed on codes are not compiled. These allow the user to give details on what happens in the function. Comments are good reminders on what the code is all about and for what. Comments also help other developers to understand what the code when they look at it.

To make a comment, add a /* at the beginning of the comment. End the written comment with a */. When commenting, comment on everything except the basic portions of the code, where explanations are no longer necessary because the meanings are already clearly understood.

Also, comments can be utilized for quick removal of code parts without having to delete them. Just enclose portions of the code in /* */, then compile. Remove these tags if these portions are to be added back into the code.

USING VARIABLES

Understanding variables

Define the variables before using them. Some common ones include char, float and int.

Declaring variables

Again, variables have to be declared before the program can use them. To declare, enter data type and then the name of the variable. Take a look at these examples:

> char name;

> float x;

> int f, g, i, j;

Multiple variables can also be declared all on a single line, on condition that all of them belong to the same data type. Just separate the names of the variables commas (i.e., int f, g, i, j;).

When declaring variables, always end the line with a semicolon to denote that the line has ended.

Location on declaring the variables

Declaring variables is done at the start of the code block. This is the portion of the code enclosed by the brackets {}. The program won't function well if variables are declared later within the code block.

Variables for storing user input

Simple programs can be written using variables. These programs will store inputs of the user. Simple programs will use the function scanf, which searches the user's input for particular values. Take a look at this example:

```
#include <stdio.h>


int main()

{

int x;


printf( "45: " );

scanf( "%d", &x );

printf( "45 %d", x );

getchar();

return 0;

}
```

The string &d informs the function scanf to search the input for any integers.

The command & placed before the x variable informs the function scanf where it can search for the specific variable so that the function can change it. It also informs the function to store the defined integer within the variable.

The last printf tells the compiler to read back the integer input into the screen as a feedback for the user to check.

Manipulating variables

Mathematical expressions can be used, which allow users to manipulate stored variables. When using mathematical expressions, it is most important to remember to use the "=" distinction. A single = will set the variable's value. A == (double equal sign) is placed when the goal is to compare the values on both sides of the sign, to check if the values are equal.

For example:

x = 2 * 4; /* sets the value of "x" to 2 * 4, or 8 */

x = x + 8; /* adds 8 to the original "x " value, and defines the new "x" value as the specific variable */

x == 18; /* determines if the value of "x" is equal to 18 */

x < 11; /* determines if the "x" value is lower than 11 */

CONDITIONAL STATEMENTS

Conditional statements can also be used within the C program. In fact, most programs are driven by these statements. These are determined as either False or True and then acted upon depending on the results. The most widely used and basic conditional statement is if.

In C, False and True statements are treated differently. Statements that are "TRUE" are those that end up equal to nonzero numbers. For example, when a comparison is performed, the outcome is a "TRUE" statement if the returned numerical value is "1". The result is a "FALSE" statement if the value that returns is "0".

Basic conditional operators

The operation of conditional statements is based on mathematical operators used in comparing values. The most common conditional operators include the following:

< /* less than */

6 < 15 TRUE

> /* greater than */

10 > 5 TRUE

<= /* less than or equal to */

4 <= 8 TRUE

>= /* greater than or equal to */

8 >= 8 TRUE

!= /* not equal to */

4 != 5 TRUE

== /* equal to */

7 == 7 TRUE

How to write a basic "IF" conditional statement

A conditional "IF" statement is used in determining what the next step in the program is after evaluation of the statement. These can be combined with other types of conditional statements in order to create multiple and powerful options.

Take a look at this example:

```
#include <stdio.h>


int main()

{

 if ( 4 < 7 )

  printf( "4 is less than 7");

  getchar();

}
```

The "ELSE/ELSE IF" statements

These statements can be used in expanding the conditional statements. Build upon the "IF" statements with "ELSE" and "ELSE IF" type of conditional statements, which will handle different types of results. An "ELSE" statement will be run when the IF statement result is FALSE. An "ELSE IF" statement will allow for the inclusion of multiple IF statements in one code block, which will handle all the various cases of the statement.

Take a look at this example:

```c
#include <stdio.h>

int main()
{
  int age;

  printf( "Please type current age: " );
  scanf( "%d", &age );
  if ( age <= 10 ) {
    printf( "You are just a kid!\n" );
  }
  else if ( age < 30 ) {
    printf( "Being a young adult is pretty awesome!\n" );
  }
  else if ( age < 50 ) {
    printf( "You are young at heart!\n" );
  }
  else {
    printf( "Age comes with wisdom.\n" );
  }
  return 0;
```

```
}
```

The above program will take all the input from the user and will run it through the different defined IF statements. If the input (number) satisfies the 1st IF statement, the 1st printf statement will be returned. If it does not, then input will be run through each of the "ELSE IF" statements until a match is found. If after all the "ELSE IF" statements have been run and nothing works, the input will be run through the "ELSE" statement at the last part of the program.

LOOPS

Loops are among the most important parts of C programming. These allow the user to repeat code blocks until particular conditions have been met. Loops make implementing repeated actions easy and reduce the need to write new conditional statements each time.

There are 3 main types of loops in C programming. These are FOR, WHILE and Do... WHILE.

"FOR" Loop

The "FOR" loop is the most useful and commonly used type of loop in C programming. This loop continues to run the function until the conditions set for this loop are met. There are 3 conditions required by the FOR loop. These include initialization of the variable, meeting the condition and how updating of the variable is done. All of these conditions need not be met at the same time, but a blank space with semicolon is still needed to prevent the loop from running continuously.

Take a look at this example:

```
#include <stdio.h>


int main()

{

 int y;


 for ( y = 0; y < 10; y++;){
```

```
    printf( "%d\n", y );

}

getchar();

}
```

The value of y has been set to 0, and the loop is programmed to continue running as long as the y value remains less than 10. At each run (loop), the y value is increased by 1 before the loop is repeated. Hence, once the value of y is equivalent to 10 (after 10 loops), the above loop will then break.

WHILE Loop

These are simpler than the FOR loops. There is only one condition, which is that as long as the condition remains TRUE, the loop continues to run. Variables need not to be initialized or updated, but can be done within the loop's main body.

Take a look at this example:

```
#include <stdio.h>

int main()

{

int y;


while ( y <= 20 ){

    printf( "%d\n", y );

    y++;

}
```

```
getchar();

}
```

In the above program, the command y++ will add 1 to the variable *y* for each execution of the loop. When the value of *y* reaches 21, the loop will break.

DO...WHILE Loop

This is a very useful loop to ensure at least 1 run. FOR and WHILE loops check the conditions at the start of the loop, which ensures that it could not immediately pass and fail. DO...WHILE loops will check the conditions when the loop is finished. This ensures that the loop will run at last once before a pass and fail occurs.

Take a look at this example:

```
#include <stdio.h>

int main()

{

int y;

y = 10;

do {

printf("This loop is running!\n");

} while ( y != 10 );

getchar();

}
```

This type of loop displays the message whether the condition results turn out TRUE or FALSE. The *y* variable is set to 10. The WHILE loop has been set to run

when the y value is not equal to 10, at which the loop ends. The message was
printed because the condition is not checked until the loop has ended.

The WHILE portion of the DO..WHILE loop must end with a semicolon. This is
also the only instance when a loop ends this way.

Conclusion

Thank you again for purchasing this book!

I hope this book was able to help you to understand the complex terms and language used in C. this programming method can put off a lot of users because of its seemingly complexity. However, with the right basic knowledge, soon, you will be programming more complex things with C.

The next step is to start executing these examples. Reading and understanding this book is not enough, although this will push you into the right direction. Execution will cement the knowledge and give you the skill and deeper understanding of C.

Finally, if you enjoyed this book, please take the time to share your thoughts and post a review on Amazon. We do our best to reach out to readers and provide the best value we can. Your positive review will help us achieve that. It'd be greatly appreciated!

Thank you and good luck!

Book 2
C++ Programming Professional
Made Easy

BY SAM KEY

Expert C++ Programming Language
Success in a Day for Any Computer
User!

Programming Box Set #18: C Programming Professional Made Easy & C++ Programming Professional Made Ease

Table Of Contents

Introduction

I want to thank you and congratulate you for purchasing the book, "Professional C++ Programming Made Easy".

This book contains proven steps and strategies on how to learn the C++ programming language as well as its applications.

There's no need to be a professional developer to code quick and simple C++ programs. With this book, anyone with basic computer knowledge can explore and enjoy the power of the *C++ Programming Language*. Included are the following fundamental topics for any beginner to start coding *today:*

- The basic C++ terms

- Understanding the C++ Program Structure

- Working with Variables, Expressions, and Operators

- Using the Input and Output Stream for User Interaction

- Creating Logical Comparisons

- Creating Loops and Using Condition Statements

- And Many More!

Thanks again for purchasing this book, I hope you enjoy it!

Chapter 1 – Introduction to C++

What You Will Learn:

**A Brief History of the C++ Language

**C++ Basic Terminology

**C++ Program Structure

C++ is one of the most popular programming languages that people are using today. More specifically, C++ is a library of "commands" that tell your computer what to do and how to do it. These commands make up the *C++ source code.*

Take note that C++ is different from the *C* programming language that came before it. In fact, it is supposedly better version of the C language when *Bjarne Stroustrup* created it back in 1983.

Even today, the C++ language serves as the "starting point" for many experts in the world of programming. Although it is particularly easy to learn and apply, the ceiling for C++ mastery is incredibly high.

C++ Basic Terminology

Of course, the first step in learning the C++ programming language is to understand the basic terms. To prevent any unnecessary confusion at any point as you read this book, this section explains the most commonly used terms in the C++ program syntax. Just like the entire programming language itself, most terms in C++ are easy to remember and understand.

Compiler

Before anything else, take note that a compiler is needed to run the codes you've written with C++. Think of compilers as "translators" that convert programming language into *machine language* – the language that a computer understands. The machine language consists of only two characters (1s and 0s), which is why it is also called as *binary language*. If you're learning C++ at school, then you shouldn't worry about getting a compiler for C++ *or* an *Integrated Development Environment* for that matter.

Integrated Development Environment

An Integrated Development Environment (IDE) is essentially the software you're using to write C++ programs. It only makes sense for IDEs to come with compilers needed to run your codes. If you have no experience with C++ programming and attempting to learn it on your own, you can opt for a free C++ IDE such as *Code::Blocks*. A good choice for complete beginners is to opt for a simple C++ IDE such as *Quincy 2005* since there is very little setup required.

Variables and Parameters

Variables are individual blocks in the program's memory that contains a given value. A value may be set as a constant, determined by the value of other variables using operators, or set/changed through user input. Variables are denoted by variable names or *identifiers*. In programming with C++, you can use any variable name you desire as long as all characters are valid. Remember that only alphanumeric characters and "underscores" (_) can be used in identifiers. Punctuation marks and other symbols are not allowed.

Keep in mind that variables always need to be *declared* first before they can be used. Declaring variables are different from deciding their actual values; meaning both processes are done in two different codes. These processes will be explained in the next chapter.

"Parameters" work the same way as regular variables. In fact, they are even written in the same syntax. However, parameters and variables are initialized in different ways. Parameters are specifically included in *functions* to allow arguments to be passed to a separate location from which the functions are called.

Statements

Every program written with C++ consists of different lines of code that performs tasks such as setting variables, calling functions, and other expressions. These lines are *statements*. Each individual statement always ends with a semicolon (;). More importantly, statements in a function are executed chronologically based on which comes first. Of course, this order can be altered using *flow control statements* such as "if statements" and "loops".

Functions

Functions are blocks in a C++ program structured to complete a single task. You can call upon functions at any point whilst the program is running. Curly brackets or braces ({}) enclose the statements or "body" in each function. Aside from a function name, functions are also set with corresponding "types" which refer to the requested form of *returned value*. You can also use and set parameters at the beginning of each function. They are enclosed in parentheses "()" and separated using commas (,).

In C++, the following is the most used syntax when creating functions:

"type" "name" (parameter 1, parameter 2, parameter 3, ...)

```
{
        "statements";
}
```

Comments

When working on particularly bigger projects, most experienced programmers use "comments" that can be used as descriptions for specific sections in a C++ program. Comments are completely ignored by a compiler and can therefore ignore proper coding syntax. Comments are preceded either by a *two slashes* (//) or a *slash-asterisk* (/*). You will find comments in the examples throughout this book to help you understand them. A quick example would be the *"Hello World!"* program below. Of course, you can also use comments in your future projects for reference and debugging purposes.

The C++ Program Structure

The program structure of C++ is very easy to understand. The compiler reads every line of code from top to bottom. This is why the first part of a C++ program usually starts with *preprocessor directives* and the declaration of variables and their values. The best way to illustrate this structure is to use the most popular example in the world of C++ -- the "Hello World!" program. Take note of the lines of code as well as the comments below:

#include <iostream> // this is a preprocessor directive

int main() // this line initiates the function named main, which should be found in every C++ program

{

   std::cout << "Hello World!"; // the statements found between the curly braces make up the main function's body

return 0; // the return 0; statement is required to tell the program that the function ran correctly. However, some compilers do not require this line in the main function

}

The topmost line ("#include <iostream>") is a preprocessor directive that defines a section of the standard C++ programming library known as the Input/Output Stream or simply *iostream*. This section handles the input and output operations in C++ programs. Remember that this is important if you wish to use "std::cout" in the main function's body.

The first line "int main ()" initializes the main function. Remember that the "int" refers to the *integer* data type and he "main" refers to the function's name. There are other data types aside from int. But you should focus on the integer data type for now. Since the "Hello World!" program does not need a parameter, it leaves the space between the parentheses succeeding the function name blank. Also, bear in mind that you should NOT place a semicolon (;) after initializing functions.

Next is the function's body, denoted by the open curly brace. This particular part ("std::cout") of the program refers to the **standard character output** device, which is the computer's display device. Next comes the *insertion operator* (<<) from the input/output stream which means the rest of the line is to be outputted (excluding quotations). Lastly, the statement is closed with a semicolon (;).

The last line in the function's body is the *return statement* ("return = 0;"). Remember that the return expression (in this example, "0") depends on the data type specified upon initialization of the function. However, it is possible to create functions without the need for return statements using the "void" function type. For example; *void main ()*.

An alternate way to do this is to include the line "using namespace std;" under the preprocessor line so you no longer need to write "std::" each time you use it. If you opt for this method, the code would look like:

```
#include <iostream>

using namespace std;

int main()

{

        cout << "Hello World!";

        return 0;

}
```

Chapter 2 – C++ Variables and Operators

What You Will Learn:

**Introduction to C++ Operators and How to Use Them

**Declaring and Determining the Value of Variables

**Creating New Lines in the Program Output

In a C++ program, variables and constants are controlled or "operated" using *Operators*. Take note that the basic operators in the C++ programming language are essentially the same as arithmetic operator. This includes the equal sign (=) for assigning expressions, the plus sign (+) for addition, the minus sign (-) for subtraction, the asterisk (*) for multiplication, the forward slash (/) for division, and the percentage sign (%) for obtaining the remainder from any expression.

C++ also uses other operators to fulfill additional tasks other than basic arithmetic operations. As mentioned in the previous chapter, the iostream header allowed you to use the insertion operator (<<) for processing output. There are also different operators accessible even without the #include directive. These "basic" operators can be categorized under *increment/decrement operators, comparison operators, compound assignment operators,* and *logical operators.*

Declaring Variables

Before using variables in C++ operations, you must first declare them and determine their values. Again, declaring variables and giving their values are two separate processes. The syntax for declaring variables are as follows:

"type" "variable";

Just like when initializing functions, you need to specify the data type to be used for a given variable. For example; say you want to declare "x" as an integer variable. The initialization should look like this:

int x;

After the declaration of x, you can give it a value using the assign operator (=). For example; to assign the value "99" to variable x, use the following line:

x = 99;

Make sure to declare a variable first before you assign a value to it. Alternatively, you can declare a variable and assign a value to it using a single line. This can be done using:

int x = 99;

Aside from setting these expressions as you write the program, you can also use operations and user input to determine their values as the program runs. But first, you need to learn about the other operators in C++.

Increment and Decrement Operators

The increment operator consists of two plus signs (++) while the decrement operator consists of two minus signs (--). The main purpose of increment and decrement operators is to shorten the expression of adding and subtracting 1 from any given variable. For example; if x = 2, then ++x should equal 3 while −x should equal 1.

If being used to determine the values of two or more variables, increment and decrement operators can be included as either a prefix or suffix. When used as a suffix (x++ or x--), it denotes the original value of x *before* adding or subtracting 1. When run on their own, both ++x and x++ have the same meaning. But when used in setting other variables, the difference is made obvious. Here is a simple example to illustrate the difference:

X = 5;

Y = ++x;

In this example, the value of y is determined *after* increasing the value of x. In other words, the value of y in this example is equal to 6.

X = 5;

Y = x++;

In this example, the value of y is determined *before* increasing the value of x. In other words, the value of y in this example is equal to 6.

Compound Assignment Operators

Aside from basic arithmetic operators and the standard assignment operator (=), compound assignment operators can also be used to perform an operation before a value is assigned. Compound assignment operators are basically shortened versions of normal expressions that use basic arithmetic operators.

Here are some examples of compound assignment operators:

x -= 1; // this is the same as the expression x = x − 1;

x *= y; // this is the same as the expression x = x * y;

x += 1;   // this is the same as the expression x = x + 1;

x /= y;   // this is the same as the expression x = x / y;

Comparison Operators

Variables and other expressions can be compared using relational or comparison operators. These operators are used to check whether a value is greater than, less than, or equal to another. Here are the comparison operators used in C++ and their description:

==   -   checks if the values are equal

<   -   checks if the first value is less than the second

>   -   checks if the first value is greater than the second

<=   -   checks if the first value is less than *or* equal to the second

>=   -   checks if the first value is greater than *or* equal to the second

!=   -   checks if the values are NOT equal

Comparison operators are commonly used in creating condition statements. They can also be used to evaluate an expression and return a *Boolean value* ("true" or "false"). Using the comparison operators listed above; here are some example expressions and their corresponding Boolean value:

(8 == 1) // this line evaluates to "false"

(8 > 1) // this line evaluates to "true"

(8 != 1) // this line evaluates to "true"

(8 <= 1) // this line evaluates to "false"

Also take note that the Boolean value "false" is equivalent to "0" while "true" is equivalent to other non-zero integers.

Aside from numerical values, the value of variables can also be checked when using comparison operators. Simply use a variable's identifier when creating the expression. Of course, the variable must be declared and given an identified value first before a valid comparison can be made. Here is an example scenario

```
#include <iostream>
using namespace std;

int main ()

{
    int a = 3;     // the values of a and b are set first
    int b = 4;
    cout << "Comparison a < b = " << (a < b);
    return 0;
}
```

The output for this code is as follows:

Comparison a < b = true

Take note that the insertion operator (<<) is used to insert the value of the expression "a < b" in the output statement, which is denoted in the 7th line ("cout << "Comparison a < b = "..."). Don't forget that you *need an output statement* in order to see if your code works. The following code will produce no errors, but it won't produce an output either:

```
#include <iostream>

int main (

{
    int a = 3;
    int b = 4;
    (a < b);
```

   return 0;

}

In this code, it is also true that a < b. However, no output will be produced since the lines necessary for the program output are omitted.

Logical Operators

There are also other logical operators in C++ that can determine the values of Boolean data. They are the NOT (!), AND (&&), and OR (||) operators. Here are specific examples on how they are used:

!(6 > 2)   // the **NOT** operator (!) completely reverses any relational expressions and produces the opposite result. This expression is false because 6 > 2 is correct

(6 > 2 && 5 < 10) // the **AND** (&&) operator only produces true if both expressions correct. This expression is true because both 6 > 2 && 5 < 10 are correct

(6 = 2 || 5 < 10) // the **OR** (||) operator produces true if one of the expressions are correct. This expression is true because the 5 < 10 is correct although 6 = 2 is false.

You can also use the NOT operator in addition to the other two logical operators. For example:

!(6 = 2 || 5 < 10) // this expression is false

!(6 > 2 && 5 < 10) // this expression is also false

!(6 < 2 && 5 < 10) // this expression is true

Creating New Lines

From this point on in this book, you will be introduced to simple C++ programs that produce output with multiple lines. To create new lines when producing output, all you need to do is to use the *new line character* (\n). Alternatively, you can use the "endl;" manipulator to create new lines when using the "cout" code. The main difference is that the *internal buffer* for the output stream is "flushed" whenever you use the "endl;" manipulator with "cout". Here are examples on how to use both:

cout << "Sentence number one \nSentence number two";

The example above uses the new line character.

cout << "Sentence number one" << endl;
cout << "Sentence number two";

The example above uses "endl;".

Of course, the first code (using \n) is relatively simpler and easier for general output purposes. Both will produce the following output:

Sentence number one

Sentence number two

Chapter 3 – All About User Input

What You Will Learn:

**Utilizing the Input Stream

**Using Input to Determine or Modify Values

**How to Input and Output Strings

Up to this point, you've learned how to make a C++ program that can perform arithmetic operations, comparisons, and can produce output as well. This time, you will learn how to code one of the most important aspects of computer programs – *user input*.

As stated earlier, user input can be utilized to determine or modify the values of certain variables. C++ programs use abstractions known as *streams* to handle input and output. Since you already know about the syntax for output ("cout"), it's time to learn about the syntax for input ("cin").

The Extraction Operator

The input syntax "cin" is used with the *extraction operator* (>>) for formatted input. This combination along with the *keyboard* is the standard input for most program environments. Remember that you still need to declare a variable first before input can be made. Here is a simple example:

int x; // this line declares the variable identifier x. Take note of the data type "int" which means that only an integer value is accepted

cin >> x;   // this line extracts input from the cin syntax and stores it to x

User input can also be requested for multiple variables in a single line. For example; say you want to store integer values for variables x and y. This should look like:

int x, y;   // this line declares the two variables

cin >> x >> y;   // this line extracts user input for variables x and y

Take note that the program will automatically require the user to input *two* values for the two variables. Which comes first depends on the order of the variables in the line (in this case, input for variable "x" is requested first).

Here is an example of a program that extracts user input and produces an output:

#include <iostream>   // again, this is essential for input and output
using namespace std;

int main ()

{

    int x;
    cout << "Insert a random number \n";
    cin >> x;   // this is where user input is extracted
    cout << "You inserted: " << x;
    return 0;

}

Bear in mind that the value extracted from the input stream overwrites any initial value of a variable. For example, if the variable was declared as "int x = 2;" but was later followed by the statement "cin >> x;", the new value will then replace the original value until the program/function restarts or if an assignment statement is introduced.

Strings

Keep in mind that there are other types you can assign to variables in C++. Aside from integers, another fundamental type is the *string*. A string is basically a variable type that can store sets of characters in a specific sequence. In other words, this is how you can assign words or sentences as values for certain variables.

First of all, you need to add the preprocessor directive "#include <string>" before you can use strings in your program. Next, you need to declare a string before it can receive assignments. For example; if you want to declare a string for "Name" and assign a value for it, you can use the code:

```
#include <string>
using namespace std;

int main ()

{
   string name;
   name =  "Insert your name here"; // including quotations

}
```

Creating output using strings is basically the same as with integers. You only need to use "cout" and insert the string to the line. The correct syntax is as follows:

string name;

Name = "Your Name Here";

cout << "My name is: " << name;

Without any changes, the output for the above code is:

Your Name Here

Inputting Strings

To allow user input values for strings, you need to use the function "getline" in addition to the standard input stream "cin". The syntax for this is "getline (cin, [string]);". Below is an example program that puts string input into application.

```
#include <iostream>
#include <string>
using namespace std;

int main ()

{
        string name;
        cout << "Greetings! What is your name?\n";
        getline (cin, name); // this is the extraction syntax
        cout << "Welcome " << name;
        return 0;

}
```

Take note that strings have "blank" values by default. This means nothing will be printed if no value is assigned or if there is no user input.

Chapter 4 – Using Flow Control Statements

What You Will Learn:

**If and Else Selection Statements

**Creating Choices

**Creating Iterating/Looping Statements

Remember that statements are the basic building blocks of a program written using C++. Each and every line that contains expressions such as a variable declaration, an operation, or an input extraction is a statement.

However, these statements are *linear* without some form of flow control that can establish the "sense" or "logic" behind a C++ program. This is why you should learn how to utilize flow control statements such as *selection statements* and *looping statements*.

If and Else Statements

If and else statements are the most basic form of logic in a C++ program. Basically, the main purpose of an "if" statement is to allow the execution of a specific line or "block" of multiple statements only *if* a specified condition is fulfilled.

Next is the "else" statement which allows you to specify what would occur in case the conditions aren't met. Without an "else" statement, everything inside the "if" statement will be completely ignored. Here the syntax for an "if" and "else" statement:

if (age >= 18)

      cout << "You are allowed to drink.";

else

      cout << "You are not yet allowed to drink.";

Remember that conditions can only be set using comparison operators and logical operators (refer to Chapter 2). Take note that you can also execute multiple statements using if/else conditions by enclosing the lines in curly braces. It is also possible to use composite conditions using logical operators such as AND (&&) and OR (||).

Finally, you can use another "if" statement after an "else" statement for even more possibilities. Of course, you also need to specify conditions for every "if" statement you use. Here is a good example that demonstrates what you can do using "if" and "else" statements in addition to user input:

```
#include <iostream>
using namespace std;

int main()

{
    int number;
    cout << "Enter a number from 1-3\n";
    cin >> number;
    if (number == 1 || number == 2)
        cout << "You have entered either 1 or 2.";
    else if (number == 3)
        cout << "You have entered 3.";
```

```
        else
        {
                cout << "Please follow the instructions\n";
                cout << "Please Try Again.";
        }
        return 0;
}
```

There are 3 possible outcomes in the program above. The first outcome is achieved if the user entered any of the numbers 1 or 2. The second outcome is achieved if the user entered the number 3. Lastly, the third outcome is achieved if the user entered a different number other the ones specified.

Creating Choices (Yes or No)

Another way to utilize if/else statements is to create "Yes or No" choices. For this, you need to make use of the variable type "char" which can hold a character from the *8-bit character set* (you can use char16_t, char32_t, or wchar_t for larger character sets; but this is not usually necessary). Just like all other variables, a "char" variable needs to be declared before it can be used.

Of course, you want the user to make the choice, which is why you need to use the "cin" function to extract user input. Here is a simple program that asks for the user's gender:

```
#include <iostream>
using namespace std;

int main()

{
        char gender; // this is the char variable declaration
```

```
cout << "Male or Female? (M/F)";
cin >> gender; // user input is stored to gender
if (gender == 'm' || gender == 'M')
        cout << "You have selected Male.";
else if (gender == 'f' || gender == 'F')
        cout << "You have selected Female.";
else
        cout << "Please follow the instructions.";
return 0;

}
```

Take note that you should use *single quotation marks* (') when pinpointing "char" values. In C++, "char" values are always called inside single quotation marks. Additionally, remember that "char" values are case-sensitive, which is why the example above used the OR (||) operator in the conditions to accept both lowercase and uppercase answers. You can see that the program above checked if the user entered 'm', 'M', 'f', or 'F'.

Looping Statements

Lastly, using "loops" allow statements to be executed for a set number of times or until a condition is met. By incorporating other statements in loops, you can do far more than just create pointless repetitions. But first, you need to be familiar with the different types of loops.

There are 3 types of loops in C++ -- *while, do,* and *for.*

While Loop

The "*while loop*" is regarded as the simplest form of loop in the C++. Basically, it repeats the statement(s) as long as the given condition is true. Keep in mind that

57

your code should be structured to eventually fulfill the condition; otherwise you might create an "infinite loop".

Here is an example of a while loop:

int x = 100;

while (x >= 0)   // the condition for the loop is set
```
    {
    cout << x;
    --x;    // the value of x is decreased
    }
```

In this example, the loop executes as long as the value of x is greater than or equal to 0. Take note of the decrement operator (--) in the statement "--x;". This makes sure that the value of x is continually decreased until the condition is met and the loop ends.

Do-While Loop

The next type of loop is the *"do-while loop"*. The do-while loop is essentially the same as the while loop. The main difference is that the do-while loop allows the execution of the statement(s) at least *once* before the condition is checked. Whereas in the while loop, the condition is checked *first*.

Here is an example of a do-while loop:

int x = 100;
int y;

do
```
    {
    cout << "The value is " << x << "\n";
```

```
cout << "Enter a value to subtract.";
cin >> y;
x -= y;
}
```
while (x > 0);   // in the do-while loop, the condition is checked last

In the example above, the statements are executed at least once before the value of x is checked. Whereas in a while loop, there is a possibility that the statement(s) will not be executed at all.

For Loop

The third type of loop is the *"for loop"* which has specific areas for the *initialization, condition,* and *increase.* These three sections are sequentially executed throughout the life cycle of the loop. By structure, for loops are created to run a certain number of times because increment or decrement operators are usually used in the "increase" section.

Here is the syntax for this loop to help you understand it better:

```
for (int x = 10; x > 0; x--)
```

Notice the three expressions inside the parentheses (int x = 10; x > 0; x--) are separated in semicolons. These parameters denote the three sections of the loop. You may also use multiple expressions for each section using a comma (,). Here is the syntax for this:

```
for ( int x = 10, y = 0; x != y; --x, ++y )
    {
    cout << "X and Y is different\n";
    }
```

In this example, the loop is executed as long as x is not equal to y. And in order for the loop to end, the values of x and y are adjusted until the value of x equals the value of y. Based on the parameters above, the statement "X and Y is different" will run a total of 5 times before the loop is ended.

Conclusion

Thank you again for purchasing this book!

I hope this book was able to help you to learn and understand the C++ programming language!

The next step is to start from where you are now and try to learn something new. Keep in mind that you've only scratched the surface of all the things you can do in the world of C++!

Finally, if you enjoyed this book, please take the time to share your thoughts and post a review on Amazon. We do our best to reach out to readers and provide the best value we can. Your positive review will help us achieve that. It'd be greatly appreciated!

Thank you and good luck!

Check Out My Other Books

Below you'll find some of my other popular books that are popular on Amazon and Kindle as well. Simply click on the links below to check them out. Alternatively, you can visit my author page on Amazon to see other work done by me.

C Programming Success in a Day

Android Programming in a Day

Python Programming in a Day

PHP Programming Professional Made Easy

CSS Programming Professional Made Easy

C Programming Professional Made Easy

HTML Professional Programming Made Easy

JavaScript Programming Made Easy

**Programming Box Set #18: C Programming Professional Made Easy & C++
Programming Professional Made Ease**

Windows 8 Tips for Beginners

If the links do not work, for whatever reason, you can simply search for these titles on the Amazon website to find them.